I'M IN THE BAND

PERFORMING Live

Richard Spilsbury

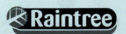

Raintree is an imprint of Capstone Global Library Limited, a company incorporated in England and Wales having its registered office at 7 Pilgrim Street, London, EC4V 6LB – Registered company number: 6695582

www.raintreepublishers.co.uk
myorders@raintreepublishers.co.uk

Edited by Clare Lewis, Mandy Robbins, Penny West and James Benefield
Designed by Steve Mead
Original illustrations © Capstone Global Library Ltd 2015
Picture research by Ruth Blair
Production by Victoria Fitzgerald
Originated by Capstone Global Library Ltd
Printed and bound in China by CTPS

ISBN 978 1 406 28249 8 (hardback)
18 17 16 15 14
10 9 8 7 6 5 4 3 2 1

Acknowledgements
We would like to thank the following for permission to reproduce photographs: Corbis pp. 6 (© Radius Images), 12 (© Bettmann), 31 (© Albert Pena/Cal Sport Media/ZUMAPRESS.com); Getty Images pp. 4 (Jose Luis Pelaez), 7 (Ian Dickson/Redferns), 8 bottom (Mick Hutson/Redferns), 9 (Chris Schmidt), 10 (PNC), 11 (Photodisc), 13 (GAB Archive/Redferns), 15 (Simone Joyner/Contributor), 16 (L. Busacca/WireImage for J Records), 21 top (Kevin Steele), 22 (Image Source), 23 (Jay Blakesberg), 25 (Julian Parker/UK Press), 26 (Steve Granitz/WireImage), 27 (Hill Street Studios), 29 (Dave Wright/MCT/MCT), 30 (Simone Joyner), 32 (Cultura/Marcel Weber), 33 (DreamPictures), 34 (AFP PHOTO / Alejandro PAGNI), 35 (Alexandro Auler/LatinContent), 38 (Oleg Prikhodko), 39 (Ryan McVay); iStock pp. 5 (© monkeybusinessimages); Shutterstock pp. 8 top (MJTH), 17 bottom (iofoto), 17 top (rawcaptured), 19 (Pavel L Photo and Video), 21 bottom (Vladyslav Danilin), 24 (Faraways), 28 (bikeriderlondon), 36 (trekandshoot), 37 (Stokkete).

Artistic Effects: Shutterstock.

Cover photograph reproduced with permission of Getty Images (Robin Little/Redferns).

We would like to thank Matt Anniss for his invaluable help in the preparation of this book.

CONTENTS

Why perform live? 4

What are you going to play? 6

Getting ready to rock 14

Finding gigs 20

Preparing for a gig 26

Stepping out on stage 36

From the backroom to the big stage! 40

Quiz 42

Glossary 44

Find out more 46

Index 48

why perform Live?

If you are in a band, you are probably thinking about performing your first live gig. That is a great idea! Most bands find that the excitement of playing songs to an enthusiastic audience helps them to take their music to a whole new level.

why play live?
- To have fun.
- To find fans. No one hears you play at home! And fans tell friends and get you more fans!
- To become a performer. Playing live takes practice and you get better the more you do.
- To improve your playing. The pressure of a gig makes you rehearse really hard.

YOU HAVE ROCKED YOUR BEDROOM FOR LONG ENOUGH. IT IS TIME TO PLAY TO A CROWD.

Playing live is vital for a newly formed band. It helps band members to focus on how and what they play and it makes them pull together as a team. And if you really have a dream of making it big, performing live could get you noticed. When a band's live shows create a buzz, reporters, music journalists and promoters hear about them and that is when the rise to the top begins.

What you need to perform
✓ Other people who love music as much as you do
✓ Instruments and sound equipment
✓ A place to practise
✓ A way of getting your gear to rehearsals and gigs
✓ Lots of ideas for songs

WHAT ARE YOU GOING TO PLAY?

Before you can think about performing, you need some songs to play! Many bands start out singing covers — songs written and made famous by other bands . But it is great to learn how to write songs and develop your own sound.

The great cover-up

Plenty of bands get together just to play other people's songs. There is nothing wrong with that. The band UB4 first became popular in the United States in 1983 with *Labour of Love*, an album of cover songs. Some bands do a combination of original tunes and covers. They wow the crowd with a familiar song and then slip in somethin original to see how that goes down.

IF YOU PLAY COVERS FOR FREE, OR IF MONEY YOU EARN IS USED FOR CHARITABLE OR EDUCATIONAL PURPOSES, YOU DO NOT NEED PERMISSION TO PLAY THEM.

The art of songwriting

There are no rules about writing songs. You can write the lyrics (the words) first, the melody, or write the melody and the lyrics at roughly the same time. Songwriters don't just wake up with an idea for a song and write it in a matter of minutes. You might suddenly get an idea for some lyrics or a tune in your head, but it takes a lot of work to turn those ideas into a finished song.

It is said Robert Plant wrote the lyrics to "Stairway to Heaven" in 15 minutes. But Led Zeppelin bandmate Jimmy Page had spent two weeks before that working out the guitar parts!

Did you know?

LED ZEPPELIN PERFORMING LIVE ON STAGE.

BANDSPEAK

Don't be a copycat!

Songwriters take out copyright on songs, which means they own the music, the lyrics or sometimes both. Be careful not to pass off another artist's song as your own.

Writing lyrics

To help get you started in songwriting, listen to as much music as you can. Think about the melodies, the lyrics and the way the songs are structured. How have songwriters used combinations of instruments or rhythms to create different moods?

Inspiration

Songwriters get inspiration in different ways. It might be a line or image in a book, a news report or a film that sparks an idea, or even something they overheard on a bus! Many songwriters write about things they are feeling or things that have happened to them. Keep a notepad and pen with you at all times so you can jot down good ideas when they come to you.

I would walk 40 minutes to school and back [in] any weather, and my little way of dealing with that was just sort of sing ... So for me the line blurs so easily between music and nature because that's almost like the same thing for me.

Björk, on being inspired by nature in her songs

Song structures

Songs usually have several verses. Most of the time, the lines rhyme. Each verse is different. Together they can tell the story or describe the subject of the song. The chorus is the part of the song repeated after each verse. A catchy chorus should express the title or central idea of the song and stay in listeners' heads after they hear it!

Stages in writing lyrics

1. Find inspiration.

2. Write a first verse that introduces the story or theme of the song.

3. Write a catchy chorus that you will repeat after each verse.

4. Write the rest of the song, perhaps following one of these two basic structures: Verse, Verse, Chorus, Verse or Chorus, Verse, Chorus. The final verse could finish off the story of your song.

5. Come up with a good title for your completed song.

SOME SONGWRITERS PREFER TO WORK ALONE. OTHERS ENJOY WORKING IN PAIRS SO THEY CAN SPARK IDEAS OFF EACH OTHER.

Writing tunes

You don't have to be an expert on your instrument to write great songs. Sit at the piano or pick up a guitar and experiment until you find a series of notes or a tune that sounds good!

Writing a score

Jot down the note combinations that you like in a music paper notebook. Or you can use a MIDI keyboard. This can be hooked up to a computer, so you can play the tune on the keyboard and use a program to turn the sounds into notes that you can print onto sheet music.

BAND TECH: USING SOFTWARE

You can write songs without knowing how to play an instrument. Music apps like GarageBand have drum, guitar and keyboard loops you can use to create a track. Software packages like Band-in-a-Box allow you to type in a chord progression and select a musical style and tempo to create a song.

Once you have come up with the main melody, you need to colour in the background of your song with some chords. Chords are groups of notes you play behind the melody to create the harmonies and mood of the song. It is those repeating chord patterns that make songs good to listen to and cheerful, scary, exciting or sad. If you can't play chords on an instrument, work with a friend who can.

BandSpeak

Chords

Chords are three or more notes played together at the same time. They are either upbeat (major) or sad (minor). You will be able to play most songs if you learn six simple chords on a guitar or keyboard: C, D minor, E minor, F, G and A minor.

SOME BANDS JAM TOGETHER IN ORDER TO HELP THEM WRITE SONGS BASED ON A RIFF ONE MEMBER CAME UP WITH.

INSPIRED

Lennon and McCartney

John Lennon and Paul McCartney wrote some of the most popular songs in rock and roll history. Together they penned most of the Beatles' greatest hits, such as "She Loves You" and "I Want to Hold Your Hand".

The hugely successful songwriting duo met when Paul saw John's band playing at a church fête in Liverpool in 1956. They began writing songs together a year later. They often skived off school and spent the days at Paul's house writing lyrics to melodies they made up on the piano while Paul's dad was out at work.

All the better songs that we have written — the ones that anybody wants to hear — those were co-written... sometimes half the words are written by me and he'll finish them off. We go along a word each, practically.

John Lennon,
speaking in 1963

PAUL McCARTNEY (LEFT) AND JOHN LENNON (RIGHT) WERE FOUNDING MEMBERS OF THE BEATLES.

In some songwriting teams, one person writes the music and the other writes the lyrics, but Lennon and McCartney both wrote words and music on their collaborations. If one came up with an initial idea, the other would help them flesh out the tune or complete the lyrics. Many people think their slightly different approaches are what make their songs great. John's ideas for songs were often about personal experiences or politics, while Paul told more optimistic, made-up stories in his songs, often about love.

The Beatles' bestselling songs

"I Want to Hold Your Hand"	1963	12 million
"Can't Buy Me Love"	1964	8 million
"Hey Jude"	1968	7 million

FANS OF THE BEATLES SCREAMED SO LOUDLY THAT IT WAS HARD TO HEAR THE MUSIC OVER THEIR NOISE.

GETTING READY TO ROCK

It is often said that to be successful in the music business takes 5 per cent inspiration and 95 per cent perspiration. Before you take one step towards that stage, your band needs to rehearse – big time.

Where and when?

First you need a rehearsal space, ideally somewhere free where the neighbours won't hear you. You can try a garage, garden shed or cellar. Ask the owners first, obviously! Then you all need to work out a realistic rehearsal schedule. It helps to agree on a regular time, as everyone is more likely to remember it.

> We have a regular schedule that calls for rehearsals on the week nights. That way, everyone can tend to personal obligations during the day, and be able to fully concentrate on rehearsals later. Sometimes we start at 6.00 p.m. and take it to 12.00 a.m. — and often beyond.

Wayne Coyne, vocalist/guitarist of the Flaming Lips

Record your sessions

You could record some of your rehearsal sessions. Listening to yourselves play helps you spot the areas that need work and the parts that sound great! You don't need expensive equipment to do this. You could just use a microphone and a laptop. If you record songs onto a computer you can convert them into MP3 files. Then the person doing the recording can send these to the rest of the band to use as jam tracks for practising at home.

BAND TECH: RECORD ON THE MOVE

Some bands buy a small digital stereo recorder to record the band in a variety of situations, including rehearsals and at gigs in small venues. They use SD and Compact Flash cards to store music and transfer data and they are easy to take anywhere because they are portable and powered by batteries.

Make rehearsals count

There are a few things you can do to get the best out of band rehearsals. For one thing – have fun! When bands enjoy playing together, they sound better. Next, everyone should practise their parts for the songs at home so they arrive ready to play. It also saves time if bandmates with extra gear get there early to set up, otherwise time is wasted while the drummer tightens every peg on the kit!

Pre-rehearsal checklist
• Practice space booked?
• List of songs that will be rehearsed sent to all band mates?
• Does everyone know which parts to practise?
• Drinks and snacks for half-time chill out?

BANDS THAT PLAY TOGETHER REGULARLY MIGHT ONLY DO A COUPLE OF WEEKS' INTENSE REHEARSING BEFORE A TOUR, BUT MOST REHEARSE HARD FOR SIX TO EIGHT WEEKS BEFORE BIG PERFORMANCES.

It's all in the timing

Rehearsals are vital. Even easy tunes take a while to memorize and even an experienced band usually has to play a song at least 20 times to nail it. Rehearsals also help with the tricky issue of tempo. Tempo is the speed or timing of music. Tempo can be slow, fast or in-between and some songs include changes of tempo. Bands need to rehearse so that everyone plays the songs at the same tempo and at the tempo that is right for each song!

BAND TECH: METRONOMES

A metronome is a device that keeps regular beats and can help bands keep the tempo of a song in rehearsals. Mechanical metronomes are adjusted by hand. You can also get electronic metronomes, software that turns computers into metronomes or you can download metronome apps.

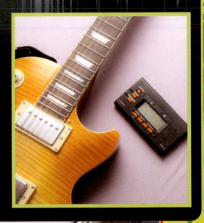

GETTING YOUR TIMING RIGHT MEANS THE WHOLE BAND ENDS A SONG AT THE SAME TIME.

Set lists

A set list is a list of songs that a band plans to perform at a gig. It lists the songs in order so that everyone knows what to play and when.

Most bands vary set lists depending on the audience, where the gig will be and how long they will play. So, if a band were playing at a school disco, they would play upbeat dance numbers. If they were playing background music for a family barbeque, they would probably play a mellower set.

Changing tempo

Bands compile set lists carefully to entertain and keep audiences interested. Choose songs with different tempos to create changes in mood, such as two fast songs then one slow song, and so on. Use changes in dynamics too. Dynamics means the volume of your playing. If you play at full volume the whole time, the set will sound a bit boring and hurt the audience's ears!

BANDSPEAK

Tag games

One way to compile a set list:

1. Write song titles on tags (strips of paper).
2. Arrange the tags in a random line and play the songs in that order.
3. Rearrange the tags and play the line-ups till you find which set list works best.

...I find that the sets that work best for us start out being really hard, and then go into a mellow section where the audience can breathe, then pump up again with more intensity, and finally end with something melodic to send the audience home happy.

Stephen Perkins, drummer for punk/metal/rock band Jane's Addiction

THE LAST SONG OF THE SET IS USUALLY YOUR BEST-KNOWN SONG. HAVING A GOOD CLOSING SONG IS SO IMPORTANT THAT SOME BANDS CHOOSE THE LAST SONG OF THEIR SET FIRST!

FINDING GIGS

When rehearsals are going well and you have a set list of songs you can perform, it is time to find some gigs so you can unleash your amazing band on the world!

People won't just come up and offer you gigs, especially at first. You have to get out and find them. Scan school and community notice boards for adverts about talent shows and concerts. Is there a school or youth group function your band could play at? Ask friends and family if they know of any parties or events you could play at, too.

<u>Book yourself</u>
Having trouble getting a gig? Put on your own.
1. Find a venue for free if you can, or hire a hall.
2. Invite other bands. They can help to advertise it and help get a good turnout.
3. Rock the house!

YOU MAY HAVE TO PLAY GIGS FOR FREE AT FIRST. IT'S A GOOD CHANCE TO SHARPEN UP YOUR MATERIAL.

Managing the band

Many bands hire a manager to book their gigs, or choose one bandmate to do it. Venues like to deal with one person to avoid mixing up dates and other details of the performance. Maybe you have a persuasive friend who would be willing to act as your band manager or perhaps a helpful adult could do the job?

BandSpeak

Doing demos

Bands get shows by making demos and sending these to people. Demos are CDs with samples of songs. These allow the organizers to see if the music suits their event. If you make demos, put your name and contact details on the CD so those who hear it can get in touch.

Gearing up to go

When you have booked a gig, find out about the venue. Ask how big it is, and what kind of equipment and sound systems it has. Check if the venue has a sound person to make sure the audience can hear the band.

Not every venue needs a sound system. When bands play in places like a small café or at an event in a single room, they might not need any help being heard. But in larger venues, bands use equipment such as amplifiers to make their music loud and clear.

AN AMPLIFIER BOOSTS SOUND FROM AN INSTRUMENT.

BAND TECH: AMP IT UP!

An amplifier is an electronic device that makes sounds louder. For example, a pickup collects sound signals from an electric guitar. The signals travel down a cable to an amplifier. The amplifier interprets the signals and sends them through a speaker at a volume an audience can hear.

Gear needs

Your band will probably perform in venues that have the gear you need. Some items of kit are definite must-haves so your singer, guitar and bass are loud enough to match the drums:

- **PA (Public Announcement) system:** Singers need a PA system consisting of a microphone, a voice amplifier and a speaker.
- **Microphones:** You can amplify your instruments through mics on stands. You can also attach pickups or mics to your instruments.
- **Cables:** You need cables to connect the mics and/or pickups to the amplifier.

Some audio equipment shops hire out equipment. This helps bands save money and gives them the chance to see what gear is best for them.

Did you Know?

DON'T FORGET THE BASICS WHEN GETTING GEAR TOGETHER, SUCH AS SHEET MUSIC, EQUIPMENT STANDS AND MAYBE A PLACE TO CLIP YOUR SET LIST.

Getting the word out

When you have booked a gig, you want to make sure plenty of people turn up. That way you are more likely to be asked to play again and to get other gigs. So, how do you get the word out?

Word-of-mouth is the best way of getting people to come to your gig. Tell everyone you know to spread the word about the gig. Design and print flyers and posters and pass them out all over town. Create a website or web page about the band and upcoming gigs.

BAND TECH: MUSIC ONLINE

Lots of bands get known by putting music on online networking websites like Soundcloud or Bandcamp where people can download songs for free. If you try this, just remember not to give out personal information. Never meet up with people you have only communicated with online.

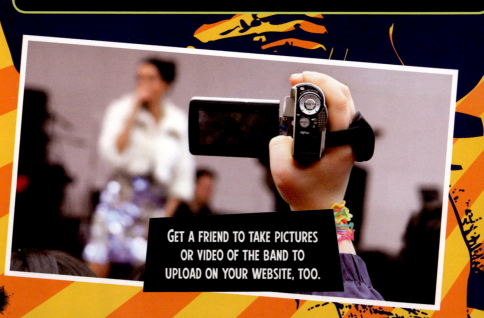

GET A FRIEND TO TAKE PICTURES OR VIDEO OF THE BAND TO UPLOAD ON YOUR WEBSITE, TOO.

Milk the merchandise

Band merchandise, such as hoodies, caps or wristbands with band names or pictures on, helps to promote a band and earn money. Lots of major bands earn more money from sales of merchandise than they do from gigs! Try to design a band logo or use band photos to print some posters, stickers and badges. You can then sell or give them away at gigs to get your name out there.

Under the guidance of famous manager Simon Cowell, the boy band One Direction made almost £100 million from 2010 to 2012 from the sale of their music and merchandising. Things sold include dolls, calendars, jumpers, duvet covers, jewellery and phone covers!

Did you know?

PREPARING FOR A GIG

People go to gigs to see bands perform. If they only wanted to hear the music, they would save their cash and listen to it at home! The best bands create a show people want to see by carefully preparing the way they look and act on stage.

Bring on the banter

Good stage banter can win fans over. Pick a spokesperson – someone who will do most of the talking to the audience. This is often the singer or lead guitarist, but can be anyone. Some people just say whatever comes into their head, but most performers plan things to say.

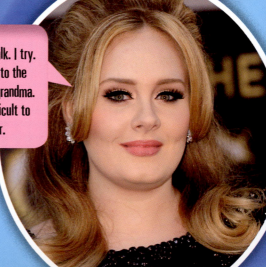

I get so nervous on stage I can't help but talk. I try. I try telling my brain: stop sending words to the mouth. But I get nervous and turn into my grandma. Behind the eyes it's pure fear. I find it difficult to believe I'm going to be able to deliver.

Adele

Speak up

Think about the way you talk as well as what you say. If you mumble into the microphone, people won't listen. Speak loudly and clearly and aim your voice towards the back of the audience. You will get more confident the more you do this. Until then, fake it. Acting confident can make people believe you are confident.

BUILD UP CONFIDENCE BEFORE A GIG BY SPENDING TIME IN FRONT OF ANY AUDIENCES YOU CAN, FROM SPEAKING IN ASSEMBLIES TO JOINING A DRAMA CLUB.

Do
- ✓ Introduce yourself and tell people who you are.
- ✓ Practise well, but not so much that it sounds fake.
- ✓ Introduce the next song, your bandmates or tell a joke or story.

Don't
- ✗ Leave long silences between songs that bore your audience.
- ✗ Make fun of other band members.
- ✗ Insult members of the audience.

Involve the audience

Involving the audience takes more than stage banter. To make people feel like part of the show, look interested. Stand up straight and tall and avoid turning your back to the audience. Look into the eyes of as many audience members as you can while performing to get and keep their attention.

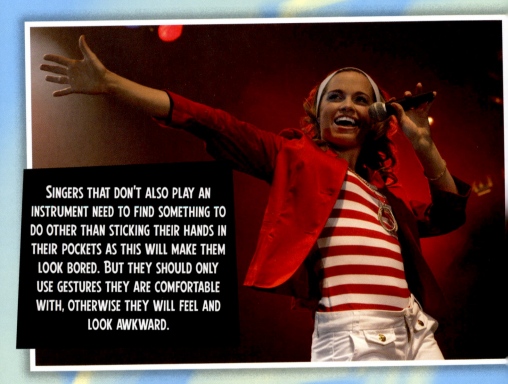

SINGERS THAT DON'T ALSO PLAY AN INSTRUMENT NEED TO FIND SOMETHING TO DO OTHER THAN STICKING THEIR HANDS IN THEIR POCKETS AS THIS WILL MAKE THEM LOOK BORED. BUT THEY SHOULD ONLY USE GESTURES THEY ARE COMFORTABLE WITH, OTHERWISE THEY WILL FEEL AND LOOK AWKWARD.

BANDSPEAK

Sing-a-longs

This is your chance to prove why a catchy chorus is so important. If it is easy to remember, you will be able to get the crowd singing it along with you. You will soon have the crowd eating out of the palm of your hand.

Show some emotion!

Try to put lots of emotion into every chord or beat you play and every word you sing. It helps if singers can try to match their facial expressions to the mood of the song. This makes the audience really listen to the words and feel like you are engaged with what you are singing.

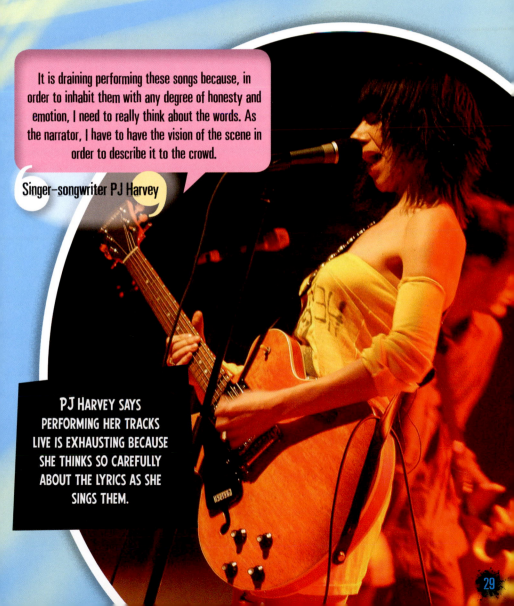

It is draining performing these songs because, in order to inhabit them with any degree of honesty and emotion, I need to really think about the words. As the narrator, I have to have the vision of the scene in order to describe it to the crowd.

Singer-songwriter PJ Harvey

PJ HARVEY SAYS PERFORMING HER TRACKS LIVE IS EXHAUSTING BECAUSE SHE THINKS SO CAREFULLY ABOUT THE LYRICS AS SHE SINGS THEM.

Putting on a show

It is boring to watch a band that acts like a group of zombies, hunched over their instruments and staring at the floor. When you are on stage, get moving. Move in a way that feels right to you and that matches the style of your music. Sway in time to a mellow tune, clap your hands to a beat, dance, jump up and down, whatever – just bring the stage to life.

BANDSPEAK

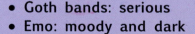

What's your style?
Different musical styles often have different stage styles too, but like all rules, these can be broken!

- Pop: coordinated dance moves
- Punk rock: shout and get in people's faces
- Folk: serious and political, or more polite
- Hard rockers: rowdy
- Goth bands: serious
- Emo: moody and dark

POP BANDS LIKE JLS OFTEN REHEARSE SOME SLICK DANCE MOVES TO ENTERTAIN THEIR FANS AND GET THEM DANCING, TOO.

Crank it up!

Some bands wear wild costumes or use things like smoke effects, props and backdrops, ladders and platforms to add interest to their stage show. There are some things you can try that won't break the bank. A bit of coloured lighting can make any band look like rock stars. You can use overhead projectors to beam designs or images onto the back of the stage or even use videos as backdrops. Watch some band performances on TV, the internet or live for ideas, too.

Did you Know?

On Coldplay's 2012 Mylo Xyloto tour, the band gave each concert-goer a Xyloband, with LED lights that were controlled by a laptop. As the music played, the wristbands flashed in time with the music and different color bands flashed at different times. It created a colorful light show in the audience.

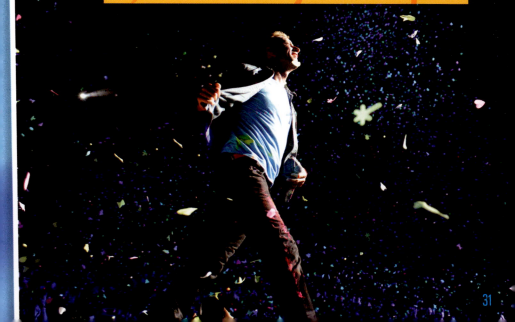

A Final run-through

When you have got a big gig coming up, make time for a final run-through of your full set list in front of a small group of close family and friends. Pretend you are playing your live show and run through the entire set as if it were the actual performance. Use your set list to guide you.

Band Tech: FILM YOURSELF!

Use a video recorder, or even your phone, to film your run-through. Then watch the performance later to see if you can spot areas for improvement. Hopefully, you will love it and watching yourselves on video will give you a boost!

GET A FRIEND OR ADULT TO FILM YOU OR YOUR BAND. WATCH IT BACK AND LEARN!

Make the best of it

To make the best of your run-through:

- Play the whole set without stopping. If someone screws up, work through it.
- Include introductions and links you plan to say between songs.
- Get the audience to stand back so they can tell if you are playing loudly enough.
- Ask for honest feedback.
- Time how long it takes to play to check your set is the right length.

BANDSPEAK

Encore?

Encores happen when the fans keep cheering for a band at the end of a gig. The band comes out to play another song or two. Even if they fake surprise, most bands plan which songs to do as their encores, so why not have an encore song ready too? Just don't rely on getting the chance to do it!

TRY OUT THE CLOTHES YOU PLAN TO WEAR TO CHECK THEY ARE COMFORTABLE, WON'T RIP WHEN YOU DANCE AND MAKE YOU LOOK COOL, NOT CLUELESS!

INSPIRED

KISS

American hard rock group KISS rose to stardom in the 1970s and soon became known for their explosive, crowd-pleasing stage shows. Their elaborate live performances feature fire breathing, smoking guitars, shooting rockets and even "flying" drum kits. In 2013, gigs for their Monster World Tour involved a giant robotic spider with glowing eyes that moved across the stage. It lifted band members into the air and shot fireballs from its legs!

Did you know?

Worldwide sales of KISS records exceed 100 million, making them one of the bestselling bands of all time!

KISS TOOK THEIR LIVE SHOWS TO A WHOLE OTHER LEVEL DURING THEIR 2013 MONSTER WORLD TOUR. YOU MIGHT NOT HAVE THE MONEY TO DO THIS, BUT IT'S ALWAYS GOOD TO MAKE AN IMPRESSION!

At live shows, KISS get the crowd chanting and joining in on songs and they challenge two sides of a room to see which can make the most noise. They become larger-than-life characters on stage with their flamboyant outfits, platform boots and striking black and white face paint. Each band member has face paint designs to match their comic book-style stage names, such as The Demon (Gene Simmons) and The Starchild (Paul Stanley).

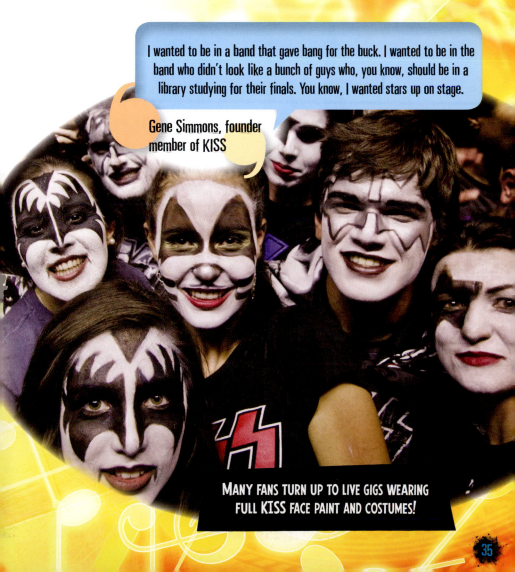

I wanted to be in a band that gave bang for the buck. I wanted to be in the band who didn't look like a bunch of guys who, you know, should be in a library studying for their finals. You know, I wanted stars up on stage.

Gene Simmons, founder member of KISS

MANY FANS TURN UP TO LIVE GIGS WEARING FULL KISS FACE PAINT AND COSTUMES!

STEPPING OUT ON STAGE

So, here you are — about to step onto a real stage for the first time. You have worked hard to get to this point, selecting bandmates, writing songs, practising and practising, and finally getting a gig. Now is the moment of truth.

Warming up

Before you go on, make sure your instruments are tuned up and that you have everything you need. Singers need to warm up their voices before performing. Hum "Do Re Mi Fa So La Ti Do", low to high and high to low, or gently sing alternate high notes and low ones, even if it sounds silly!

Checklist of things to bring to gig
- Set list
- Guitar strap, picks, spare guitar strings
- Tuner
- Cables, mics and amps
- Music stand and music sheets if needed
- Water, to drink — it gets hot on stage!

Stage Fright

Worried you might get struck down by stage fright? Everybody feels nervous before performing. Nervous energy can be a good thing because it fires you up. If you need to keep nerves in check, repeat confidence-boosting words to yourself, like "You can do it!", or get a pep talk from a parent or a friend. Fake feeling confident until you feel it for real.

Keep calm and carry on! Try this breathing exercise to help you relax:

1. Close your mouth and breathe in through the nose deeply. Hold this breath for five seconds.

2. Then breathe out slowly through the mouth. Keep doing this until you feel calmer.

SOME PERFORMERS LISTEN TO A FAVOURITE TRACK TO GET THEMSELVES IN THE MOOD FOR A SHOW.

On stage and on fire

As you turn on the mic, plug in your guitar or click your drumsticks together to signal the first tune, revel in the moment. You are on stage! Enjoy yourself.

Messing up

Have fun, even if someone makes a mistake. Every band member messes up at some point. Just get back on track as quickly as possible. If something goes wrong, the golden rule for bands is to follow what the singer or lead guitarist does.

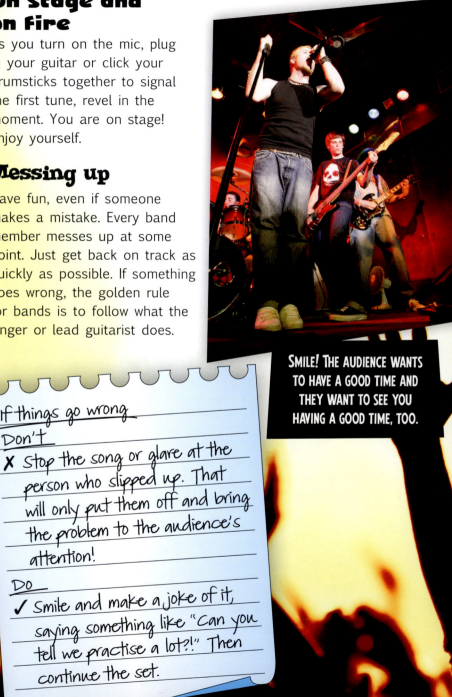

SMILE! THE AUDIENCE WANTS TO HAVE A GOOD TIME AND THEY WANT TO SEE YOU HAVING A GOOD TIME, TOO.

If things go wrong

Don't

✗ Stop the song or glare at the person who slipped up. That will only put them off and bring the problem to the audience's attention!

Do

✓ Smile and make a joke of it, saying something like "Can you tell we practise a lot?!" Then continue the set.

Celebrate!

Your first performance should raise the roof and wow the crowd. Take a bow and congratulate each other. After you have packed up your gear, mingle with the audience to soak up their praise and hear their comments. Even if it does not go totally to plan, don't be hard on yourselves. Celebrate the fact that you got the gig together and had a great time performing.

Things to do after the gig
- Have a party to celebrate!
- Assess how it went. How did the audience respond? How did you feel?
- Thank anyone who helped with moving gear, transport or anything else.
- Contact the venue manager to thank them for the gig.
- Ask about future gigs.

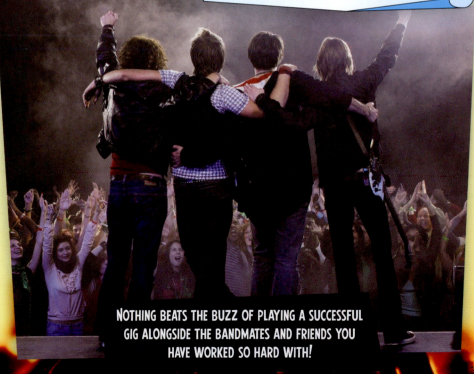

NOTHING BEATS THE BUZZ OF PLAYING A SUCCESSFUL GIG ALONGSIDE THE BANDMATES AND FRIENDS YOU HAVE WORKED SO HARD WITH!

From the back room to the big stage!

Follow these steps and you will soon find yourself stepping out of the rehearsal room ... and stepping on to the big stage!

Start out by playing covers to find your style.

Get inspiration for some lyrics for your songs.

Write tunes to go with your lyrics. Use chords and harmonies to set the right mood.

Work on the chorus until it is genuinely catchy and you can't get it out of your head.

Pick one band member or find a friend or parent to act as band manager.

Find a rehearsal space.

Plan a rehearsal schedule and get everyone to agree to it.

Come up with a set list. Don't rush this. Take time to make it great.

Design a logo and come up with some merchandise, from posters to T-shirts.

Plan and rehearse some introductions and banter for your stage show. Leave nothing to chance!

Advertise the gig anywhere and everywhere you can.

Plan dance routines or other ways to entertain and engage the audience.

Check the sound equipment at the venue or hire your own.

Decide on what you will wear at the gig.

Book a gig.

Do a demo and upload it to the internet and send it to potential venues.

Come up with stage effects or at least a backdrop for the show that tells the audience your name.

You made it to the venue: go through your sound check and warm-up and get ready to wow that crowd!

Have a final run-through in front of a friendly audience who can give you feedback.

Sort out a van to get you to the venue. Make a checklist of what you will need — and don't forget to use it.

QUIZ

Take this quiz to find out if you are ready for your first gig!

1 Has the band rehearsed together?
- **a)** Yes, twice a week for months.
- b) Yes, but we don't really have a fixed rehearsal schedule.
- c) No, we haven't found anywhere to rehearse together yet.

2 Do you play covers or your own material?
- **a)** We play a mix of covers and our own stuff.
- b) We play covers but we give them our own twist.
- c) What is a cover?

3 What shape is your set list in?
- **a)** We have got a set list for two 45-minute sets that end with a real crowd-pleaser.
- b) We have got lots of songs we can play, but not a set list yet.
- c) We can only play two songs so far.

4 How do you work on tempo?
- **a)** We have been working with a metronome to get our timing right.
- b) The singer keeps time and we follow.
- c) We like a free sound so don't worry about stuff like playing in time...

5 Have you done a demo?
- **a)** Yes, and we have uploaded it onto the internet.
- b) Yes, we just need to do something with it.
- c) No, we lost the digital recorder we borrowed.

6 Will you wear anything special on stage?
- **a)** Yes, we have gone for a style that matches the music we play.
- b) We are sticking to our normal clothes.
- c) We can't decide on a style because we don't know the kind of music we will play yet.

7 Where will you play your first gig?
- **a)** We have booked the school hall and we are advertising a free show to get people interested.
- b) We are hoping to play at a friend's birthday party next month.
- c) We are waiting to see if anyone shows interest in our demo ... when we eventually make one.

8 How will you advertise the gig?
- **a)** We have written a feature for our local newspaper.
- b) We have already designed the posters.
- c) We will just let the word get out. We have got better things to do than pin up posters.

9 What will you do if you get stage fright?
- **a)** Not going to happen – we are too well-prepared.
- b) Some breathing exercises and get a pep talk from my best mate.
- c) Run!

10 What about after the gig?
- **a)** We will be busy preparing for the next!
- b) Celebrate and get some feedback from the audience.
- c) I can't even think about that – we have got to get a gig first...

Answers

IF YOU ANSWERED MOSTLY AS: You are ready with a capital R! There is nothing to stop you getting out there and wowing the crowd. You are confident, well-rehearsed, your set list is sorted and you have thought everything through to the last detail. The only thing left to do is get in the van!

IF YOU ANSWERED MOSTLY BS: You are knocking on the door of the venue and almost feel ready to go in. But you know what – just go for it. Your band is playing well together and you have a clear idea of what and how you want to play your material. Just go ahead and book that first gig. Having that deadline will make you sort out the final details in ample time. So, what are you waiting for?

IF YOU ANSWERED MOSTLY CS: Really? Did you even read this book? Actually, you know what? I suspect you are only reading this answer out of interest. If you have formed a band and you are planning to perform live you can't really be this unprepared. So, stop reading ... and get playing!

Glossary

amplifier electronic device that makes sounds louder

banter lively and funny chat or conversation

chord two or more notes (or pitches) played together

chorus part of the song repeated after each verse

copyright document giving someone the sole right to publish and sell musical or artistic work

cover to record or perform a song originally written or performed by someone else; also, the name of a song that you cover

demo inexpensively made recording to give people an idea of what a band plays

dynamics varying levels of volume of sound in different parts of a song

encore extra song or performance at the end of a gig or show

feedback reaction to a performance

harmony combination of musical notes played at the same time to produce chords and chord progressions that sound good; also means being in agreement

lyrics words of a song

manager person who controls the activities, business dealings and other aspects of a musician's career

melody main tune of a song

merchandise products for sale linked to a band, film or television show

metronome device that produces regular ticking noises to help musicians play in time

music journalist reporter who writes about gigs and new music releases

online networking website internet platform where people who share interests can get in touch

overhead projector machine that projects enlarged images onto a wall or screen

PA system stands for public address system. A PA is an electronic amplification system used to make speech or music louder so an audience can hear it.

pickup device on a musical instrument that converts sound vibrations into electrical signals for amplification

promoter person who organizes a live performance and handles things like booking venues, tickets and publicity

rhythm strong, regular, repeated pattern of sound

riff notes that are strung together. They form a recognizable but short part of a rock song, the opening notes of a song that everyone recognizes, for instance.

set list sequence of songs that are played at a gig

sheet music handwritten or printed version of the directions for a song

stage fright fear that affects a person about to face an audience

tempo speed at which a tune or song is played

upload to take a file from your computer and put it on a website where other people can use it, and even download it

venue place where a show or gig takes place

verse group of lines that form a unit in a song or a poem

FIND OUT MORE

If you and your band want, or are preparing, to perform live you can find lots more advice on the internet, and in the books and DVDs listed here.

Go to as many live gigs as you can and watch bands and singers perform on television, the internet and on DVDs. You will get more ideas for performing live and it will get you thinking about the importance of performing rather than just playing your songs. Watch how they work the audience, and what banter they use to link songs and make a connection with their fans. As you watch, think about how you can do this, too.

To learn more first-hand about how bands plan performances and deal with things like stage fright, you could find local musicians to interview for a blog or school magazine. Ask them for any tips on how to make a performance exciting on a low or non-existent budget!

To help you with the technical side of live gigs, such as using microphones, amplifiers and other parts of sound systems, see if there are any classes you can attend at local community colleges or centres. These are also good places to meet local musicians who can tell you which music venues might be available for gigs. It's also good to get to know local musicians as they are often very supportive and helpful to new, young bands and you can learn a lot from them.

Books

Performing Live (The Music Scene), Matt Anniss (Franklin Watts, 2012)

Pop Band (Celeb), Laura Durman (Franklin Watts, 2011)

The Music Industry (The Music Scene), Matt Anniss (Franklin Watts, 2012)

You've Got Talent! (Dorling Kindersley, 2011)

Websites

www.bbc.co.uk/music/genres
Learn more about different music genres (or types of music) on this BBC website.

www.berklee.edu/careers-music-busines-management
There are lots of careers in music you could consider. This website explains a few of them.

www.gmarts.org
This web page has 10 top tips to help you when you are performing live.

teenshealth.org/teen/your_mind/problems/nerves.html
This website has tips on how to beat pre-performance nerves.

DVDs

A Hard Day's Night (1964): The first film featuring the Beatles.

Camp Rock (2008): Disney story set at a rock and roll summer camp.

Empire Records (1995): A day in the life of a record shop and its staff.

Place to visit

The British Music Experience
www.britishmusicexperience.com
This is a museum of popular music, located at the O2 in London. Using cutting edge audio-visual technology, visitors can trace historic and era-defining moments through 60 years of music history.

Index

Adele 26
after a gig 39
amplifiers 22, 23
apps 10, 17
audience involvement 28, 35
audio equipment 22, 23

banter 26, 27, 33, 38, 41
Beatles 12–13
Björk 8
breathing exercise 37

cables 23
chords 11, 40
closing songs 19
clothes 31, 33, 35, 41
co-writing 9, 12, 13
Coldplay 31
confidence 27, 37
copyright 7
covers 6, 13, 40
Cowell, Simon 25

dance moves 30, 41
demos 21, 41
digital stereo recorders 15
dynamics 18

emo 30
emotion, showing 29
encores 33
equipment checklist 36
equipment, hiring 23

face paint 35
facial expressions 29
fans 4, 33
feedback 33
first performance 36–39
Flaming Lips, The 15
flyers 24
folk 30
free, playing for 21

gestures 28
gigs, finding 20–21
Goth bands 30

hard rock 30, 34–35
harmonies 11, 40
Harvey, P J 29

inspiration for songwriting 8, 40

jamming 11, 15
Jane's Addiction 19
JLS 30

KISS 34–35

Led Zeppelin 7
Lennon, John 12–13
lighting 31
listening to music 8
logos 25, 41
lyrics 7, 8, 9, 12, 13, 29, 40

McCartney, Paul 12–13
managers 21, 25, 40
melodies 7, 8, 11, 12
merchandise 25, 41
messing up 38
metronomes 17
microphones 15, 23, 27
MIDI keyboards 10
MP3 files 15

networking websites 24

One Direction 25
online safety 24

PA (Public Announcement) systems 23
Page, Jimmy 7
Plant, Robert 7

pop 30
posters 24, 25
practising 15, 16
props 31, 34
publicity 24, 41
punk rock 30

reasons for playing live 4–5
recording songs 15
rehearsal spaces 14, 40
rehearsals 14–17, 40
riffs 11
run-through, final 32–33, 41

school functions 18, 20
set length 33
set lists 18–19, 23, 32, 40
sing-a-longs 28, 35
software 10, 17
songwriting 6, 7, 8–13, 40
sound systems 22, 23, 41
stage effects 31, 34, 41
stage fright 37

talent shows 20
team effort 5
tempos 17, 18

UB40 6

venues 20, 21, 22, 23
videos 24, 31, 32

warming up 36
word-of-mouth publicity 24

Xylobands 31